A York: Tragedy

By
Thomas Middleton

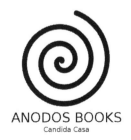

ANODOS BOOKS
Candida Casa

Thomas Middleton (1580-1627)

Originally published in 1608
Editing, cover, and internal design by Alisdair MacNoravaich for Anodos Books.
Copyright © 2017 Anodos Books. All rights reserved.

Anodos Books
1c Kings Road
Whithorn
Newton Stewart
Dumfries & Galloway
DG8 8PP

Contents

DRAMATIS PERSONAE

OLIVER ⎫
RALPH ⎬ serving-men of a house in Yorkshire
SAM   ⎭
A Boy
The WIFE
The HUSBAND
Four GENTLEMEN
A SERVANT
The MASTER of a College
The SON
A MAID
A LUSTY SERVANT
KNIGHT, a magistrate
Officers

1

SCENE I.

A house in Yorkshire.

Enter Oliver and Ralph, two serving-men.

Oliv. Sirrah Ralph, my young mistress is in such a pitiful, passionate humour[1] for the long absence of her love.

Ral. Why, can you blame her? Why, apples hanging longer on the tree then when they are ripe make so many fallings. Viz, mad wenches, because they are not gathered in time, are fain to drop of themselves, and then 'tis common, you know, for every man to take 'em up.

Oliv. Mass, thou sayest true, 'tis common indeed. But, sirrah, is neither our young master returned, nor our fellow Sam come from London?

Ral. Neither of either, as the puritan bawd says.[2] [*Noise within*] 'Slid, I hear Sam; Sam's come, here's tarry.[3] Come, i'faith, now my nose itches for news.

Oliv. And so does mine elbow.

Sam. [*Calls within*] Where are you there?

Enter Sam and a Boy.

Boy, look you walk my horse with discretion; I have rid him simply. I warrant his skin sticks to his back with very heat; if 'a should catch cold and get the cough of the lungs, I were well served, were I not?

[*Exit Boy.*

What, Ralph and Oliver!

Amb. Honest fellow Sam, welcome, i'faith! What tricks hast thou brought from London?

[*Sam is furnished with things from London which he now presents.*

Sam. You see I am hang'd after the truest fashion: three hats, and two

---

[1] Temperament, disposition.
[2] Ridiculing the affected preciseness of expression used by puritans.
[3] Delay, procrastination.

3

glasses[4] bobbling upon 'em, two rebato wires[5] upon my breast, a cap-case[6] by my side, a brush at my back, an almanac in my pocket, and three ballads in my codpiece. Nay, I am the true picture of a common serving-man.

Oliv. I'll swear thou art. Thou mayest set up when thou wilt. There's many a one begins with less, I can tell thee, that proves a rich man ere he dies. But what's the news from London, Sam?

Ral. Ay, that's well fed.[7] What's the news from London, sirrah? My young mistress keeps such a puling[8] for her love.

Sam. Why? The more fool she, ay, the more ninnyhammer[9] she.

Oliv. Why, Sam, why?

Sam. Why, he's married to another long ago.

Amb. I'faith, ye jest.

Sam. Why, did you not know that till now? Why, he's married, beats his wife, and has two or three children by her: for you must note that any woman bears the more when she is beaten.

Ral. Ay, that's true, for she bears the blows.

Oliv. Sirrah Sam, I would not for two years' wages my young mistress knew so much. She'd run upon the left hand of her wit, and ne'er be her own woman again.

Sam. And I think she was blest in her cradle, that he never came in her bed. Why, he has consumed[10] all, pawned his lands, and made his university brother stand in wax[11] for him. There's a fine phrase for a scrivener. Puh, he owes more than his skin's worth.

Oliv. Is't possible?

Sam. Nay, I'll tell you moreover he calls his wife whore as familiarly as

---

[4]Mirrors.

[5]Rebatos were frilled head-dresses, and the wires inside them kept them stiff.

[6]A traveling-case, bag, or wallet.

[7]Well asked.

[8]Whining.

[9]A fool or simpleton.

[10]Squandered.

[11]Sign a bond of debt, drawn up by a scrivener and then certified with a stamp in wax.

one would call Moll and Doll,[12] and his children bastards as naturally as can be. But what have we here? [*Pulls out two poking-sticks*] I thought 'twas somewhat pulled down my breeches: I quite forget my two poting-sticks.[13] These came from London; now anything is good here that came from London.

Oliv. Ay, farfetched,[14] you know.

Sam. But speak in your conscience, i'faith: have not we as good poting-sticks i' th' country as need to be put i' th' fire? The mind of a thing is all,[15] the mind of a thing is all. And as thou saidst e'en now, farfetched is the best thing for ladies.

Oliv. Ay, and for waiting gentlewomen, too.

Sam. But Ralph, what, is our beer sour this thunder?

Oliv. No, no, it holds countenance[16] yet.

Sam. Why then, follow me. I'll teach you the finest humour to be drunk it; I learn'd it at London last week.

Amb. Ay, faith, let's hear it, let's hear it.

Sam. The bravest humour, 'twould do a man good to be drunk in't. They call it knighting[17] in London, when they drink upon their knees.

Amb. Faith, that's excellent!

Sam. Come, follow me. I'll give you all the degrees on't in order.

[*Exeunt.*

---

[12]Names of "low" women.

[13]Poking-sticks, steel sticks used to set the plaits of the ruff.

[14]1) unusual, 2) fetched from afar; the Stationers' Register for 1566 lists a play called *Far Fetched and Dear Bought Is Good for Ladies.*

[15]This seemingly trivial utterance has important thematic ramifications regarding the Husband's psychology.

[16]Still appears to be good.

[17]A jibe at the declining standards of knighthood. Almost immediately after he was crowned, James I began conferring many new knighthoods, considered lavish and undiscriminating by those who felt that these "carpet knights" cheapened the rank.

5

SCENE II.

Outside the Husband's house, near Yorkshire

Enter Wife.

Wife. What will become of us? All will away.
My husband never ceases in expense,
Both to consume his credit and his house.
And 'tis set down by Heaven's just decree,
That riot's[18] child must needs be beggary.
Are these the virtues that his youth did promise:
Dice, and voluptuous meetings, midnight revels,
Taking his bed with surfeits, ill-beseeming
The ancient honour of his house and name?
And this not all: but that which kills me most,
When he recounts his losses and false fortunes,
The weakness of his state so much dejected,
Not as a man repentant, but half mad.
His fortunes cannot answer his expense.
He sits and sullenly locks up his arms,
Forgetting Heaven looks downward, which makes him
Appear so dreadful, that he frights my heart;
Walks heavily, as if his soul were on earth,
Not penitent for those his sins are past,
But vex'd his money cannot make them last:
A fearful melancholy, ungodly sorrow.
Oh, yonder he comes; now in despite of ills,
I'll speak to him, and I will hear him speak,
And do my best to drive it from his heart.

Enter Husband.

Husb. Pox o' th' last throw, it made
Five hundred angels vanish from my sight!
I'm damn'd, I'm damn'd: the angels[19] have forsook me!
Nay, 'tis certainly true, for he that has no coin
Is damn'd in this world: he's gone, he's gone.

Wife. Dear husband.

---

[18]Debauchery.

[19]1) gold coins worth ten shillings, with the figure of St. Michael defeating the dragon, 2) heavenly spirits; a common pun employed frequently by Middleton.

6

Husb. Oh, most punishment of all, I have a wife!

Wife. I do entreat you as you love your soul,
Tell me the cause of this your discontent.

Husb. A vengeance strip thee naked, thou art cause,
Effect, quality, property, thou, thou, thou!

[*Exit Husband.*

Wife. Bad turn'd to worse? Both beggary of the soul,
As of the body; and so much unlike
Himself at first, as if some vexed spirit
Had got his form upon him.

Enter Husband.

[*Aside*] He comes again.
He says I am the cause: I never yet
Spoke less than words of duty and of love.

Husb. [*Aside*] If marriage be honourable, then cuckolds are honourable,
for they cannot be made without marriage. Fool! What meant I to
marry to get beggars? Now must my eldest son be a knave or nothing.
He cannot live upon the soil, for he will have no land to maintain him:
that mortgage sits like a snaffle[20] upon mine inheritance, and makes me
chew upon iron. My second son must be a promoter,[21] and my third a
thief, or an underputter,[22] a slave pander. Oh beggary, beggary, to what
base uses does thou put a man!
I think the devil scorns to be a bawd:
He bears himself more proudly, has more care on's[23] credit.
Base, slavish, abject, filthy poverty!

Wife. Good sir, by all our vows I do beseech you,
Show me the true cause of your discontent.

Husb. Money, money, money, and thou must supply me!

Wife. Alas, I am the least cause of your discontent;
Yet what is mine, either in rings or jewels,
Use to your own desire. But I beseech you,

---

[20]Bridle-bit.
[21]Informer.
[22]Pander.
[23]Of his.

As y'are a gentleman by many bloods,[24]
Though I myself be out of your respect,
Think on the state of these three lovely boys
You have been father to.

Husb. Puh! Bastards, bastards,
Bastards, begot in tricks, begot in tricks!

Wife. Heaven knows how those words wrong me! But I may
Endure these griefs among a thousand more.
Oh, call to mind your lands already mortgaged,
Yourself wound into debts, your hopeful brother
At the university in bonds for you,
Like to be seiz'd upon. And--

Husb. Ha' done, thou harlot,
Whom though for fashion sake I married,
I never could abide? Thinkst thou thy words
Shall kill my pleasures? Fall off to thy friends,
Thou and thy bastards beg: I will not bate
A whit in humour.--Midnight, still I love you
And revel in your company. Curb'd in,
Shall it be said in all societies
That I broke custom, that I flagg'd in money?
No, those thy jewels I will play as freely
As when my state was fullest.

Wife. Be it so.

Husb. Nay, I protest, and take that for an earnest!

[*Spurns her.*

I will forever hold thee in contempt,
And never touch the sheets that cover thee;
But be divorc'd in bed till thou consent
Thy dowry shall be sold to give new life
Unto those pleasures which I most affect.

Wife. Sir, do but turn a gentle eye on me,
And what the law shall give me leave to do
You shall command.

Husb. Look it be done.

---

[24]Connected to many aristocratic families.

8

[Holding his hands in his pockets.

Shall I want dust and like a slave
Wear nothing in my pockets but my hands
To fill them up with nails?
Oh, much against my blood!²⁵ Let it be done;
I was never made to be a looker on.
A bawd to dice? I'll shake the drabs myself
And make 'em yield. I say, look it be done!

Wife. I take my leave; it shall.

Husb. Speedily, speedily!

[Exit Wife.

I hate the very hour I chose a wife, a trouble, trouble, three children
like three evils hang upon me! Fie, fie, fie, strumpet and bastards,
strumpet and bastards!

Enter three Gentlemen hearing him.

1st Gent. Still do those loathsome thoughts jar on your tongue,
Yourself to stain the honour of your wife,
Nobly descended. Those whom men call mad
Endanger others, but he's more than mad
That wounds himself, whose own words do proclaim
Scandals unjust, to foil his better name:
It is not fit. I pray, forsake it.

2nd Gent. Good sir, let modesty reprove you.

3rd Gent. Let honest kindness sway so much with you.

Husb. God-den,²⁶ I thank you, sir. How do you? Adieu. I'm glad to see
you. Farewell.

[Exit Gentlemen.

Instructions! Admonitions!

Enter Servant.

How now, sirrah, what would you?

---

²⁵Inclination.
²⁶Good evening.

9

Serv. Only to certify to you, sir, that my mistress was met by the way, by these who were sent for her to London[27] by her honourable uncle, your worship's late guardian.

Husb. So, sir, then she is gone and so may you be.
But let her look that the thing be done she wots[28] of,
Or Hell will stand more pleasant than her house at home.

[*Exit Servant. Enter a Fourth Gentleman.*

4th Gent. Well or ill met, I care not.

Husb. No, nor I.

4th Gent. I am come with confidence to chide you.

Husb. Who, me? Chide me? Do't finely, then: let it not move me, for if thou chid'st me, angry I shall strike.

4th Gent. Strike thine own follies, for it is they
Deserve to be well beaten. We are now in private;
There's none but thou and I. Thou'rt fond[29] and peevish,[30]
An unclean rioter, thy lands and credit
Lie now both sick of a consumption.
I am sorry for thee: that man spends with shame
That with his riches does consume his name,
And such art thou.

Husb. Peace!

4th Gent. No, thou shalt hear me further.
Thy father's and forefathers' worthy honours,
Which were our country's monuments, our grace,
Follies in thee begin now to deface.
The springtime of thy youth did fairly promise
Such a most fruitful summer to thy friends,
It scarce can enter into men's beliefs
Such dearth should hang on thee. We that see it
Are sorry to believe it. In thy change
This voice into all places will be hurl'd:
Thou and the devil have deceived the world.

---

[27]Those who were sent to conduct her to London to see her uncle.
[28]Knows.
[29]Foolish.
[30]Weak, trivial.

10

Husb. I'll not endure thee!

4th Gent. But of all the worst:
Thy virtuous wife, right honourably allied,
Thou hast proclaimed a strumpet.

Husb. Nay, then, I know thee:
Thou art her champion, thou, her private friend,[31]
The party you wot on.

4th Gent. Oh, ignoble thought!
I am past my patient blood. Shall I stand idle
And see my reputation touch'd to death?

Husb. 'T'as gall'd you this, has it?

4th Gent. No, monster, I will prove
My thoughts did only tend to virtuous love.

Husb. Love of her virtues? There it goes!

4th Gent. Base spirit,
To lay thy hate upon the fruitful honour
Of thine own bed!

> [*They draw their swords and fight, and the Husband's hurt.*

Husb. Oh!

4th Gent. Woult[32] thou yield it yet?

Husb. Sir, sir, I have not done with you.

Gent. I hope, nor ne'er shall do.

> [*Fight again.*

Husb. Have you got tricks?
Are you in cunning with me?

4th Gent. No, plain and right.
He needs no cunning that for truth doth fight.

> [*Husband is wounded and falls down.*

---

[31]Lover.

[32]A form of wilt.

11

Husb. Hard fortune, am I leveled with the ground?

4th Gent. Now, sir, you lie at mercy.

Husb. Ay, you slave!

4th Gent. Alas, that hate should bring us to our grave!
You see my sword's not thirsty for your life.
I am sorrier for your wound than yourself.
Y'are of a virtuous house: show virtuous deeds;
'Tis not your honour, 'tis your folly bleeds.
Much good has been expected in your life:
Cancel not all men's hopes. You have a wife
Kind and obedient: heap not wrongful shame
On her, your posterity. Let only sin be sore,
And by this fall, rise never to fall more.
And so I leave you.

[*Exit Gentleman.*

Husb. Has the dog left me then
After his tooth hath left me? Oh, my heart
Would fain leap after him; revenge, I say!
I'm mad to be reveng'd! My strumpet wife,
It is thy quarrel that rips thus my flesh,
And makes my breast spit blood! But thou shalt bleed.
Vanquish'd? Got down? Unable e'en to speak?
Surely 'tis want of money makes men weak.
Ay, 'twas that o'erthrew me; I'd ne'er been down else.

[*Exit.*

SCENE III.

The Husband's house, a room above.

Enter Wife in a riding suit[33] with a serving-man.

Serv. Faith, mistress, if it might not be presumption
In me to tell you so, for his excuse,
You had small reason, knowing his abuse.

---

[33]She has just returned from her uncle in London.

Wife. I grant I had, but alas,
Why should our faults at home be spread abroad?
'Tis grief enough within doors. At first sight
Mine uncle could run o'er his prodigal life
As perfectly as if his serious eye
Had numbered all his follies,
Knew of his mortgag'd lands, his friends in bonds,
Himself withered with debts; and in that minute
Had I added his usage and unkindness,
'Twould have confounded every thought of good:
Where now, fathering[34] his riots on his youth,
Which time and tame[35] experience will shake off,
Guessing his kindness to me--as I smoothed[36] him
With all the skill I had, though his deserts[37]
Are in form uglier than an unshap'd bear--
He's ready to prefer him to some office
And place at court, a good and sure relief
To all his stooping fortunes; 'twill be a means, I hope,
To make new league between us, and redeem
His virtues with his lands.

Serv. I should think so, mistress. If he should not now be kind to you
and love you, and cherish you up, I should think the devil himself kept
open house in him.

Wife. I doubt not but he will now. Prithee, leave me; I think I hear him
coming.

Serv. I am gone.

[*Exit.*

Wife. By this good means I shall preserve my lands,
And free my husband out of usurers' hands:
Now there is no need of sale. My uncle's kind;
I hope, if aught, this will content his mind.
Here comes my husband.

Enter Husband.

---

[34]Blaming.
[35]Taming, i.e., the position at court will settle him down. "Time" and "tame" are homonyms.
[36]Refined, freed from rudeness.
[37]Merits.

13

Husb. Now, are you come? Where's the money, let's see the money. Is the rubbish[38] sold, those wiseacres, your lands? Why, when! The money, where is't? Pour't down, down with it, down with it! I say, pour't o' th' ground; let's see't, let's see't!

Wife. Good sir, keep but in patience, and I hope
My words shall like you[39] well. I bring you better
Comfort than the sale of my dowry.

Husb. Hah? What's that?

Wife. Pray, do not fright me, sir, but vouchsafe me hearing. My uncle, glad of your kindness to me and mild usage--
For so I made it to him--has in pity
Of your declining fortunes, provided
A place for you at court of worth and credit,
Which so much overjoyed me.

Husb. Out on thee, filth!
Over and overjoyed, when I'm in torments?

[*Spurns her.*

Thou politic[40] whore, subtler than nine devils, was this thy journey to nuncle,[41] to set down the history of me, of my state and fortunes? Shall I that dedicated myself to pleasure be now confin'd in service to crouch and stand like an old man i' th' hams, my hat off, I that never could abide to uncover my head i' th' church, base slut?
This fruit bears thy complaints!

Wife. Oh, Heaven knows
That my complaints were praises, and best words
Of you, and your estate: only my friends
Knew of your mortgag'd lands, and were possess'd
Of every accident[42] before I came.
If thou suspect it but a plot in me
To keep my dowry, or for mine own good
Or my poor children's--though it suits a mother
To show a natural care in their reliefs,

---

[38]Land.
[39]i.e., you shall like what I have to say.
[40]Cunning.
[41]Archaic form of uncle.
[42]Particular incident.

Yet I'll forget myself to calm your blood--
Consume[43] it, as your pleasure counsels you;
And all I wish, e'en clemency affords,
Give me but comely looks and modest words.

Husb. Money, whore, money, or I'll--

[*The Husband draws his dagger.*

Enter a servant very hastily.

[*The Husband speaks to his man.*

What the devil? How now? Thy hasty news?[44]

[*Servant in a fear.*

Serv. May it please you, sir.

Husb. What? May I not look upon my dagger? Speak, villain, or I will
execute the point on thee: quick, short!

Serv. Why, sir, a gentleman from the university stays below to speak
with you.

Husb. From the university? So, university:
That long word runs through[45] me.

[*Exeunt Husband and Servant. Wife alone.*

Wife. Was ever wife so wretchedly beset?
Had not this news stepp'd in between, the point
Had offered violence to my breast.
That which some women call great misery
Would show but little here, would scarce be seen
Amongst my miseries. I may compare
For wretched fortunes with all wives that are;
Nothing will please him, until all be nothing.
He calls it slavery to be prefer'd;
A place of credit, a base servitude.
What shall become of me, and my poor children,
Two here, and one at nurse, my pretty beggars?

---

[43]Believe.

[44]i.e., news that made you come in haste.

[45]This phrase is interestingly juxtaposed to the dagger just alluded to: his brother's plight is the
one thing outside his own selfish concerns that reaches the Husband.

15

I see how ruin with a palsy hand
Begins to shake the ancient feet to dust;
The heavy weight of sorrow draws my lids
Over my dankish[46] eyes, I can scarce see.
Thus grief will last; it wakes and sleeps with me.

SCENE IV.

The Husband's house.

Enter the Husband with the Master of the College.

Husb. Pray you draw near, sir, y'are exceeding welcome.

Mast. That's my doubt, I fear; I come not to be welcome.

Husb. Yes, howsoever.

Mast. 'Tis not my fashion, sir, to dwell in long circumstance, but to be plain and effectual, therefore to the purpose. The cause of my setting forth was piteous[47] and lamentable. That hopeful young gentleman, your brother, whose virtues we all love dearly through your default and unnatural negligence, lies in bond executed for your debt, a prisoner, all his studies amazed,[48] his hope strook dead, and the pride of his youth muffled in these dark clouds of oppression.

Husb. Hum, um, um.

Mast. Oh, you have killed the towardest[49] hope of all our university! Wherefore without repentance and amends, expect ponderous and sudden judgments to fall grievously upon you. Your brother, a man who profited in his divine employments, might have made ten thousand souls fit for Heaven, now by your careless courses cast in prison which you must answer for; and assure your spirit it will come home at length.

Husb. Oh, God, oh.

---

[46]i.e., moistened with tears.
[47]1) compassionate, 2) full of piety, devout.
[48]Confounded.
[49]1) most promising, 2) of the best disposition.

16

Mast. Wifmen[50] think ill of you, others speak ill of you, no man loves you; nay, even those whom honesty condemns, condemn you. And take this from the virtuous affection I bear your brother, never look for prosperous hour, good thought, quiet sleeps, contented walks, nor anything that makes man perfect till you redeem him. What is your answer? How will you bestow[51] him? Upon desperate misery, or better hopes? I suffer till I hear your answer.

Husb. Sir, you have much wrought with me. I feel you in my soul; you are your arts' master. I never had sense till now; your syllables have cleft me. Both for your words and pains I thank you: I cannot but acknowledge grievous wrongs done to my brother, mighty, mighty, mighty wrongs. Within there?

Enter a serving-man.

Serv. Sir.

Husb. Fill me a bowl of wine.

[Exit Servant for wine.

Alas, poor brother,
Bruis'd with an execution for my sake!

Mast. A bruise indeed makes many a mortal
Sore till the grave cure 'em.

Enter Servant with wine.

Husb. Sir, I begin to[52] you; y'have chid your welcome.

Mast. I could have wish'd it better for your sake.
I pledge you, sir, to the kind man in prison.

Husb. Let it be so.

[Drink both.

Now, sir, if you please to spend but a few minutes in a walk about my grounds below, my man shall attend you. I doubt not but by that time

---

[50]Women (obs.)

[51]1) employ, dispose of (i.e., "Where is he to labor: at his studies or in jail?"), 2) possibly, give in marriage, with regard to his union with the church.

[52]Am persuaded by.

17

to be furnish'd of a sufficient[53] answer, and therein my brother fully satisfied.

Mast. Good sir, in that the angels would be pleas'd, and the world's murmurs calm'd, and I should say I set forth then upon a lucky day.

[*Exit Master with Servant.*

Husb. Oh thou confused man, thy pleasant[54] sins have undone thee, thy damnation has beggar'd thee! That Heaven should say we must not sin, and yet made women,[55] gives our senses way to find pleasure, which being found, confounds us. Why should we know those things so much misuse us? Oh, would virtue had been forbidden, we should then have proved all virtuous, for 'tis our blood to love what we are forbidden! Had not drunkenness been forbidden, what man would have been fool to a beast, and zany[56] to a swine to show tricks in the mire? What is there in three dice to make a man draw thrice three thousand acres into the compass of a round little table, and with the gentleman's palsy in the hand, shake out his posterity?[57] Thieves or beggars; 'tis done, I ha' done't, i'faith! Terrible, horrible misery! How well was I left, very well, very well! My lands showed like a full moon about me, but now the moon's i' th' last quarter, waning, waning. And I am mad to think that moon was mine: mine and my father's, and my forefathers', generations, generations. Down goes the house of us, down, down, it sinks. Now is the name a beggar, begs in me that name which hundreds of years has made this shire famous: in me, and my posterity runs out. In my seed[58] five are made miserable besides myself. My riot is now my brother's jailer, my wife's sighing, my three boys' penury, and mine own confusion.

[*Tears his hair.*

Why sit my hairs upon my cursed head?
Will not this poison scatter them?[59] Oh, my brother's
In execution among devils

---

[53]1) satisfactory, esp. in a monetary sense, 2) possibly an allusion to *Matthew* vi.34, "Sufficient unto the day is the travail thereof."

[54]Having (sensual) pleasure as their end.

[55]A feminist perspective would note that the Husband blames his wife for keeping him from his whoring, but blames his whores for keeping him from the sanctity of his home.

[56]Servant who acts as a clown.

[57]Recalls scene iii, "with a palsy hand/Begins to shake the ancient feet to dust."

[58]As a result of my actions.

[59]Some poisons were not lethal but did cause hair to fall out.

That stretch him and make him give. And I in want,
Not able for to live, nor to redeem him.
Divines and dying men may talk of Hell,
But in my heart her several torments dwell.
Slavery and misery! Who in this case
Would not take up money upon his soul,
Pawn his salvation, live at interest?
I that did ever in abundance dwell,
For me to want, exceeds the throes of Hell!

Enters his little Son with a top and a scourge.[60]

Son. What ails you, father? Are you not well? I cannot scourge my top
as long as you stand so: you take up all the room with your wide legs.
Puh, you cannot make me afear'd with this; I fear no vizards,[61] nor
bugbears.

[*Husband takes up the child by the skirts of his long coat in one hand and
draws his dagger with th' other.*

Husb. Up, sir, for here thou hast no inheritance left!

Son. Oh, what will you do, father? I am your white boy.[62]

Husb. Thou shalt be my red boy; take that!

[*Strikes him.*

Son. Oh, you hurt me, father!

Husb. My eldest beggar, thou shalt not live to ask an usurer bread, to
cry at a great man's gate, or follow "Good your honour!" by a coach;[63]
no, nor your brother. 'Tis charity to brain you.

Son. How shall I learn now my head's broke?

[*The Husband stabs him.*

Husb. Bleed, bleed, rather than beg, beg;

---

[60]A string to be used in conjunction with the top. Although this detail is taken from *Two Most
Unnatural Murders..*, I am tempted to mention these thematic *double entendres* of "scourge": 1)
a whip, 2) a cause of calamity (Attila the Hun is known as the Scourge of God), 3) one who
"lashes" vice or folly. (A scourge is also an offshoot of the main plant or tree!)

[61]Masks. The Son is mistaking his father's grimaces for playfulness.

[62]Favorite, pet, darling boy; his father makes the obvious, brutal pun.

[63]Follow a coach begging, "Good your honour!"

Be not thy name's disgrace.
Spurn thou thy fortunes first if they be base.
Come view thy second brother. Fates,
My children's blood shall spin into your faces!
You shall see
How confidently we scorn beggary!

[*Exit with his Son.*

SCENE V.

The Husband's house, the room above.

Enter a Maid with a child in her arms, the mother Wife by her asleep.

Maid. Sleep, sweet babe: sorrow makes thy mother sleep.
It bodes small good when Heaven falls so deep.[64]
Hush, pretty boy, thy hopes might have been better;
'Tis lost at dice what ancient honours won,
Hard when the father plays away the son;
Nothing but misery serves in this house.
Ruin and desolation, oh!

Enter Husband with the boy bleeding.

Husb. Whore, give me that boy!

[*Strives with her for the child.*

Maid. Oh, help, help! Out, alas! Murder, murder!

Husb. Are you gossiping, prating, sturdy quean?[65]
I'll break your clamour with your neck downstairs:
Tumble, tumble, headlong!

[*Throws her down.*

So, the surest way to charm a woman's tongue
Is break her neck: a politician did it.[66]

---

[64]i.e., someone sinks so low in evil.

[65]Impetuously brave strumpet.

[66]An allusion to the Earl of Leicester, who allegedly, in order to become available to marry Queen Elizabeth, had his first wife murdered under the guise of her having fallen down stairs and broken her neck.

Son. Mother, mother, I am kill'd, mother!

[The Wife wakes.

Wife. Ha, who's that cried? Oh me, my children!
Both, both, both bloody, bloody!

[Catches up the youngest.

Husb. Strumpet, let go the boy, let go the beggar!

Wife. Oh, my sweet husband!

Husb. Filth, harlot!

Wife. Oh, what will you do, dear husband?

Husb. Give me the bastard!

Wife. Your own sweet boy!

Husb. There are too many beggars!

Wife. Good my husband--

Husb. Dost thou prevent me still?

[Stabs at the child in her arms.

Wife. Oh God!

Husb. Have at his heart!

Wife. Oh, my dear boy!

[The Husband gets it from her.

Husb. Brat, thou shalt not live to shame thy house!

Wife. Oh Heaven!

[She's hurt and sinks down.

Husb. And perish now, be gone!
There's whores enow,[67] and want would make thee one!

Enter a Lusty Servant.

---

[67]Enough.

21

Lusty Serv. Oh, sir, what deeds are these?

Husb. Base slave, my vassal,
Comest thou between my fury to question me?

Lusty Serv. Were you the devil, I would hold you, sir.

Husb. Hold me? Presumption, I'll undo thee for't!

Lusty Serv. 'Sblood,[68] you have undone us all, sir.

Husb. Tug at[69] thy master?

Lusty Serv. Tug at a monster!

Husb. Have I no power? Shall my slave fetter me?

[*The Husband wrestles with the Servant.*

Lusty Serv. Nay then, the devil wrastles! I am thrown!

Husb. Oh, villain, now I'll tug thee, now I'll tear thee!

[*Overcomes him and kicks him with his spurs.*

Set quick spurs to my vassal, bruise him, trample him!
So, I think thou wilt not follow me in haste.
My horse stands ready saddled; away, away!
Now to my brat at nurse, my sucking beggar:
Fates, I'll not leave you one to trample on!

SCENE VI.

The Husband's house, the room below.

The Husband enters and the Master meets him.

Mast. How is't with you, sir?
Methinks you look of a distracted colour.

Husb. Who, I, sir? 'Tis but your fancy.
Please you walk in, sir, and I'll soon resolve you.

------

[68]By God's blood.
[69]Struggle with.

22

I want one small part to make up the sum,[70]
And then my brother shall rest satisfied.

Mast. I shall be glad to see it, sir. I'll attend you.

[*Exeunt.*

SCENE VII.

The Husband's house, the room above.

Lusty Serv. Oh, I am scarce able to heave up myself:
H'as so bruis'd me with his devilish weight,
And torn my flesh with his blood-hasty spur.
A man before of easy constitution
Till now, Hell's power supplied to his soul's wrong.
Oh, how damnation can make weak men strong!

Enter Master and two Servants.

Oh, the most piteous deed, sir, since you came!

Mast. A deadly greeting! Has he summ'd up this
To satisfy his brother? Here's another:
And by the bleeding infants, the dead mother!

Wife. Oh, oh!

Mast. Surgeons, surgeons! She recovers life!
One of his men all faint and bloodied!

Lusty Serv. Follow; our murderous master has took horse
To kill his child at nurse! Oh, follow quickly!

Mast. I am the readiest; it shall be my charge
To raise the town upon him!

Lusty Serv. Good sir, do follow him.

[*Exeunt Master and Servants.*

Wife. Oh, my children!

---

[70]A hidden irony in that he is off to kill his youngest child to complete the murders; the Master
realizes the double meaning early in the next scene.

23

Lusty Serv. How is it with my most afflicted mistress?

Wife. Why do I now recover? Why half live?
To see my children bleed before mine eyes,
A sight able to kill a mother's breast
Without an executioner! What, art thou mangled, too?

Lusty Serv. I, thinking to prevent what his quick mischiefs had so soon
acted, came and rush'd upon him.
We struggled, but a fouler strength than his
O'erthrew me with his arms; then did he bruise me
And rent my flesh, and robb'd me of my hair
Like a man mad in execution,
Made me unfit to rise and follow him.

Wife. What is it has beguil'd him of all grace
And stole away humanity from his breast,
To slay his children, purpos'd to kill his wife,
And spoil his servants?

Enter two Servants.

Amb. Please you, leave this most accursed place;
A surgeon waits within.

Wife. Willing to leave it.
'Tis guilty of sweet blood, innocent blood.
Murder has took this chamber with full hands,
And will ne'er out as long as the house stands.

[Exeunt.

SCENE VIII.

A road just outside Yorkshire.

Enter Husband as being thrown off his horse, and falls.

Husb. Oh, stumbling jade, the spavin[71] overtake thee, the fifty diseases
stop thee!
Oh, I am sorely bruis'd! Plague founder thee!

---

[71]A hard bony tumor or excrescence formed at the union of the splint-bone and the shank in a
horse's leg.

Thou runn'st at ease and pleasure, heart,[72] of chance
To throw me now with a flight o' th' town,
In such plain even ground! 'Sfoot,[73] a man may dice upon't, and throw
away the meadows, filthy beast!

[*Cry Within*] Follow, follow, follow!

Husb. Ha? I hear sounds of men, like hew and cry.
Up, up, and struggle to thy horse! Make on!
Dispatch that little beggar and all's done!

[*Cry Within*] Here, this way, this way!

Husb. At my back? Oh,
What fate have I! My limbs deny me go.
My will is bated; beggary claims a part.
Oh, could I here reach to the infant's heart!

*Enter Master of the College, three Gentlemen, and others with halberds.
They find him.*

All. Here, here, yonder, yonder!

Mast. Unnatural, flinty, more than barbarous:
The Scythians[74] in their marble-hearted fates
Could not have acted more remorseless deeds
In their relentless natures than these of thine!
Was this the answer I long waited on,
The satisfaction of thy prisoned brother?

Husb. Why, he can have no more on's[75] than our skins,
And some of 'em want but fleaing.

1st Gent. Great sins have made him impudent.

Mast. H'as shed so much blood that he cannot blush.

2nd Gent. Away with him; bear him along to the justice!
A gentleman of worship dwells at hand;
There shall his deeds be blaz'd.

---

[72]An exclamation, as in "'sheart!" ("by God's heart!")

[73]By God's foot.

[74]Nomadic inhabitants of an ancient region extending over a large part of European and Asiatic Russia, noted for their cruelty; Tamburlaine was a Scythian.

[75]From us.

Husb. Why, all the better.
My glory 'tis to have my action known.
I grieve for nothing, but I miss'd of one.

Mast. There's little of a father in that grief.
Bear him away.

[*Exeunt.*

SCENE IX.

The Knight's house.

Enters a Knight with two or three Gentlemen.

Kni. Endangered so his wife? Murdered his children?

4th Gent. So the cry comes.

Kni. I am sorry I e'er knew him,
That ever he took life and natural being
From such an honoured stock and fair descent
Till this black minute without stain or blemish.

4th Gent. Here come the men.

Enter the Master of the College and the rest, with the Husband prisoner.

Kni. The serpent of his house?
I'm sorry for this time that I am in place of justice.

Mast. Please you, sir.

Kni. Do not repeat it twice: I know too much.
Would it had ne'er been thought on.
Sir, I bleed for you.

4th Gent. Your father's sorrows are alive in men:
What made you show such monstrous cruelty?

Husb. In a word, sir,
I have consum'd all, play'd away Longacre,[76]
And I thought it the charitablest deed I could do

---

[76]A name applied generally to any estate.

26

To cozen[77] beggary, and knock my house o' th' head.

Kni. Oh, in a cooler blood you will repent it!

Husb. I repent now, that one's left unkill'd,
My brat at nurse. Oh, I would full fain have wean'd him!

Kni. Well, I do not think but in tomorrow's judgment
The terror will sit closer to your soul
When the dread thought of death remembers[78] you;
To further which, take this sad voice[79] from me:
Never was act play'd more unnaturally.

Husb. I thank you, sir.

Kni. Go, lead him to the jail,
Where justice claims all; there must pity fail.

Husb. Come, come, away with me.

[*Exit the Husband as prisoner.*

Mast. Sir, you deserve the worship of your place;
Would all did so: in you the law is grace.

Kni. It is my wish it should be so. Ruinous man,
The desolation of his house, the blot
Upon his predecessors' honour'd name:
That man is nearest shame that is past shame.

[*Exeunt.*

SCENE X.

Outside the Husband's house.

Enter Husband with the officers, the Master and Gentlemen as going by his house.

Husb. I am right against my house, seat of my ancestors.
I hear my wife's alive, but much endangered:

---

[77]Cheat.
[78]Is remembered by.
[79]Serious utterance.

27

Let me entreat to speak with her before
The prison gripe[80] me.

Enter his Wife brought in a chair.

1st Gent. See, here she comes of herself.

Wife. Oh, my sweet husband, my dear distressed husband,
Now in the hands of unrelenting laws,
My greatest sorrow, my extremest bleeding,
Now my soul bleeds!

Husb. How now? Kind to me? Did I not wound thee, left thee for dead?

Wife. Tut, far greater wounds did my breast feel:
Unkindness strikes a deeper wound than steel.
You have been still unkind to me.

Husb. Faith, and so I think I have.
I did my murthers roughly out of hand,
Desperate and sudden, but thou hast devis'd
A fine way now to kill me; thou hast given mine eyes
Seven wounds a piece. Now glides the devil from
Me, departs at every joint, heaves up my nails![81]
Oh, catch him! New torments that were ne'er invented!
Bind him one thousand more, you blessed angels,
In that pit bottomless![82] Let him not rise
To make men act unnatural tragedies,
To spread into a father, and in fury,
Make him his children's executioners,
Murder his wife, his servants, and who not!
For that man's dark where Heaven is quite forgot.

Wife. Oh, my repentant husband!

Husb. My dear soul, whom I too much have wrong'd,
For death I die, and for this have I long'd.

Wife. Thou shouldst not--be assured--for these faults die,
If the law could forgive as soon as I.

[Children laid out.

---

[80]Seize.

[81]With the allusion to Christ; cf. scene ii, "Wear nothing in my pockets but my hands/To fill them up with nails."

[82]cf. *Revelations* xx.1-3.

28

Husb. What sight is yonder?

Wife. Oh, our two bleeding boys laid forth upon the threshold!

Husb. Here's weight enough to make a heartstring[83] crack!
Oh, were it lawful that your pretty souls
Might look from Heaven into your father's eyes,
Then should you see the penitent glasses melt,[84]
And both your murthers shoot upon my cheeks!
But you are playing in the angels' laps,
And will not look on me,
Who, void of grace, kill'd you in beggary.
Oh, that I might my wishes now attain,
I should then wish you living were again,
Though I did beg with you, which thing I fear'd!
Oh, 'twas the enemy my eyes so blear'd![85]
Oh, would you could pray Heaven me to forgive
That will unto my end repentant live!

Wife. It makes me e'en forget all other sorrows
And leaven part with this. Come, will you go?

Husb. I'll kiss the blood I spilt and then I go:
My soul is bloodied, well may my lips be so.

[*He kisses the children.*

Farewell, dear wife, now thou and I must part;
I of thy wrongs repent me with my heart.

Wife. Oh, stay, thou shalt not go!

Husb. That's but in vain; you must see it so.
Farewell, ye bloody ashes[86] of my boys;
My punishments are their eternal joys.[87]
Let every father look into my deeds,
And then their heirs may prosper while mine bleeds.

Wife. More wretched am I now in this distress
Than former sorrows made me.

---

[83]The heart was supposedly braced with strings that could be broken with emotional stress.
[84]i.e., eyes weep.
[85]Dimmed the sight of, i.e., "The devil deceived me."
[86]Remains.
[87]i.e., "My sons will not be punished for my sins because I will expiate them."

[Exeunt Husband and Officers guarding him with halberds.

Mast. Oh kind wife, be comforted!
One joy is yet unmurdered:
You have a boy at nurse: your joy's in him.

Wife. Dearer than all is my poor husband's life.
Heaven give my body strength, which yet is faint
With much expense of blood, and I will kneel,
Sue for his life, number up all my friends
To plead for pardon my dear husband's life.

Mast. Was it in man to wound so kind a creature?
I'll ever praise a woman for thy sake.
I must return with grief, my answer's set.[88]
I shall bring news weighs heavier than the debt:
Two brothers, one in bond lies overthrown,
This on a deadlier execution.[89]

FINIS

---

[88]Fixed, as in colors setting.
[89]1) a writ in law, 2) capital punishment.

Printed in Great Britain
by Amazon

53744864R00020